STANLEY HOLLOWAY
MORE MONOLOGUES AND SONGS

Stanley Holloway, OBE, was born in 1890 and was originally a seaside concert artist. His first major appearance on
the London stage was in 1919 and since then he has
performed in scores of straight plays, musical comedies,
pantomimes, films and solo performances on both sides of
the Atlantic. He will always be remembered as Alfred P.
Doolittle in *My Fair Lady* as well as for his unparalleled
rendering of the comic monologue. Mr Holloway now lives
in Sussex, still making records and appearing on television
from time to time.

The enormous popularity of the first collection of Holloway Monologues published by Elm Tree Books in 1979 has
prompted the editor, Michael Marshall, to assemble a
second collection to mark the great entertainer's ninetieth
year. But this time, in addition to the monologues which
became Stanley Holloway's personal hallmark, Michael
Marshall has widened his selection to include the best
examples of Mr Holloway's musical comedy and his most
vivid 'turns' on the halls – many of which were previously
unpublished.

Michael Marshall is a theatrical and film historian, whose
book *Top Hat & Tails* – a biography of Jack Buchanan – was
published by Elm Tree Books in 1978. He has been the
Member of Parliament for Arundel since 1974 and is now
Parliamentary Under-Secretary of State for Industry.

Stanley Holloway
More Monologues and Songs

Edited and with an introduction by
MICHAEL MARSHALL

Illustrated by Bill Tidy

ELM TREE BOOKS/
EMI MUSIC PUBLISHING

To STANLEY and LANEY HOLLOWAY

First published in Great Britain 1980
by Elm Tree Books/Hamish Hamilton Ltd
Garden House 57–59 Long Acre London WC2E 9JZ
in association with EMI Music Publishing Ltd
138–140 Charing Cross Road London WC2H 0LD

Introduction copyright © 1980 by Michael Marshall
See also further copyright acknowledgements on page xvi

British Library Cataloguing in Publication Data

Stanley Holloway, more monologues and songs.
  1. Humorous poetry, English
  2. Humorous recitations
  3. English poetry – 20th century
  I. Marshall, Michael
  821'.07   PR1195.H8

  ISBN 0–241–10478–5

Typeset in Great Britain by
King's English Typesetters Ltd, Cambridge
and printed by
Lowe & Brydone Printers Ltd, Thetford, Norfolk

CONTENTS

Foreword by Stanley Holloway vii
Introduction by Michael Marshall viii
Notes and Acknowledgements xvi

Part I: MONOLOGUES

And Yet I Don't Know! *by R. P. Weston and Bert Lee* (1919) 1
'My Word! You Do Look Queer!' *by R. P. Weston and Bert Lee*
 (1923) 5
The Street Watchman's Story *by Charles J. Winter* (1910) 7
On Strike *by Charles Pond* (1906) 9
Evings' Dorg 'Ospital *by Charles Pond* (1906) 11
The George Lashwood Monologue *by Frank Eyton* (1942) 13
Pukka Sahib *by Reginald Purdell* (1940) 15

Part II: MUSICAL COMEDY PERFORMANCES

It'll Be All the Same *by Arthur Anderson* (1920) 21
The King who Wanted Jam for Tea *by Greatrex Newman*
 (1925) 22
Sometimes I'm Happy *by Irving Caesar and Vincent Thomas*
 (1927) 23
Keep Smiling *by Oscar Hammerstein* (1934) 25
My Missus *by Stanley Holloway* (1935) 27
Careless Talk *by Stanley Holloway and Graham John* (1940) 28
Get Me to the Church on Time *by Alan Jay Lerner* (1956) 30
Comedy Tonight *by Stephen Sondheim* (1964) 32
Wiv a Little Bit of Luck *by Alan Jay Lerner* (1956) 34
London Pride *by Noël Coward* (1969) 35

Part III: MUSIC HALL PERFORMERS

My Lord Tomnoddy – Various (early nineteenth century)   37
Goin' to the Derby – *J. W. Rowley* (1850)   39
The Dark Girl Dress'd in Blue – *Harry Clifton* (1862)   41
Act on the Square Boys – *The Great Vance* (1866)   44
A Motto for Every Man – *Arthur Lloyd* (late nineteenth century)   46
I Live in Trafalgar Square – *Morney Cash* (1902)   48
Burlington Bertie from Bow – *Ella Shields* (1914)   50
Oh, I Must Go Home Tonight! – *Billy Williams* (1908)   54
I Thowt Mebbe I Would – An' I Did – *Jack Pleasants* (1912)   56
I Went Down to Bright – *Phil Ray* (1912)   58
Champagne Charlie – *George Leybourne* (1866)   59

Part IV: HUMOROUS POETRY(Recorded in 1960)

Edward Lear – How Pleasant to Know Mr Lear   63
W. S. Gilbert – Bab Ballards:
      The Ape and The Lady   64
      The Yarn of The 'Nancy Bell'   66
      Peter the Wag   69

POSTSCRIPT Old Barty *by Douglas Grant* (1919)   73

DISCOGRAPHY   75

FOREWORD
by Stanley Holloway

When Michael Marshall collected all the 'Sam',' 'Albert' and many of my other monologues together last year, I wondered if they still had much public appeal. Well, the response was overwhelming, there were several reprints, and, apparently, the audience wanting an 'encore'.

So Michael has done it again, by collecting many more of the spoken and musical items with which I have been closely identified in my eighty years as a performer. This time he has been able to go much wider than the monologues and the items we have selected bring back many happy memories.

Little did I think, as a small boy at the start of the century, when I sat up in 'the gods' watching the great music-hall artistes that I should appear with many of them and recreate their work on record. I could hardly have guessed, too, that I would spend so many years of my life on stage, in concert party and musical comedy. Nor that films, radio and television would keep me busy into my ninetieth year.

I am sometimes asked if I have any ambitions left. As a life-long cricket lover, I feel a bit like the batsman who is entering the nervous nineties – having got this far I might as well go after the three figures and, who knows, 'Wiv a Little Bit of Luck', I might make it!

STANLEY HOLLOWAY
May 1980

INTRODUCTION
by Michael Marshall

This year marks the ninetieth birthday of Stanley Holloway; it seemed appropriate therefore to bring together a collection of material which demonstrated the versatility of this great entertainer.

In *The Stanley Holloway Monologues* – published by Elm Tree/EMI in 1979 – the stories of Sam, Albert and many additional characters created for Stanley by Marriot Edgar, Weston and Lee and other writers were brought together. The present collection enables us to look at much of Stanley Holloway's other work on the Halls, in Revue, for Musical Comedy, as a film performer and in making records. It also reflects Stanley's appreciation of the fellow artists from whom he learnt his trade.

The monologue section opens on page 1 with 'And Yet I Don't Know!' which was written by R. P. Weston and Bert Lee for the Yorkshire entertainer, Ernest Hastings. Hastings, a bald-headed man with a pince-nez, used this as a song monologue, accompanying himself on the piano. While awaiting demobilization in 1919 Stanley, just back from service with the Connaught Rangers in France, saw Hastings perform this number at the Empire Theatre, Hartlepool. He quickly learnt the words and it became useful for unaccompanied recitations at parties. It was the first true monologue that Stanley worked in variety, and he relishes and still quotes to this day the tale of the 'careful' Northerner and his agonies of decision-making in choosing a wedding present for his niece.

'My Word! You Do Look Queer!' was the other great comedy monologue in Ernest Hastings' repertoire, also written by Bob Weston and Bert Lee. After Hastings' death, Stanley made the number his own. He recorded it as recently as 1975 in an album entitled 'There's Life In the Old Dog Yet' and both the song and the album aptly sum up Stanley's impatience with self-pity.

'The Street Watchman's Story' was the opening recitation in Bransby Williams' music-hall act. Williams – known as 'The Hamlet of the Halls' – was the first great dramatic monologuist to impress Stanley when, as a boy, he saw him at the London Pavilion. 'The Street Watchman's Story' (also known as 'The 'ole In The Road') was a typical Cockney piece written by Charles J. Winter in 1910. Unusually for Bransby Williams – who specialized in the full tear-jerking Victorian dramatic recitation – the lyric is full of humour and was perfectly suited to Stanley's style when he recorded it in 1957 as an example of work on the Halls before the First World War.

'On Strike' was recorded at the same time as another sample of the Edwardian music-halls. It has a strangely contemporary flavour with its account of an early demarcation dispute. Whether its implicit male chauvinism is in keeping with modern thinking is more open to debate but Stanley made the most of Charles Pond's ironic words.

'Evings' Dorg 'Ospital' also written by Charles Pond, is yet another example of the Cockney humour of the Halls before the First World War. It must have been regarded as mildly daring in 1906 to expose the pragmatic – if not downright hypocritical – attitude of many of those who looked after other people's pets like 'Evings' (the Cockney rendition of Evans).

'The George Lashwood Monologue' was performed by Stanley in Firth Shepherd and Robert Nesbitt's Revue 'Fine and Dandy' at the Savile Theatre in 1942. The words written by Frank Eyton were a tribute to Lashwood, who had died only a few weeks earlier. A distinguished-looking man, he had been known as 'the Beau Brummel of the Halls'. As Stanley himself recalls:

Lashwood was marvellous. I'd seen him in my early days of going to the Halls. When he came on, his personality was so great that he didn't just take the stage – he took the whole theatre with him as he launched into one of his ballads, like 'Where are the Boys from the Village Tonight?'.

In recreating the Lashwood turn, Stanley came on in frock coat and top hat and performed the decline and fall of 'a Swell' whose bogus aristocratic pretensions are revealed when he describes his schooldays at Harrow *College* instead of Harrow *School*.

'Pukka Sahib' was a sketch in the previous revue at the Saville, 'Up and Doing', which opened in 1940. It drew fully on Stanley's skills as a monologuist since it was based on Bransby Williams' best-known recitation 'The Green Eye of the Little Yellow God'. Reginald Purdell's version was written for one of the Savage Club's Saturday night entertainments and Stanley suggested it as a possible item to his co-star and closest friend, Leslie Henson.

The sketch involved Stanley as a serious monologuist in full evening dress hounded to distraction by Leslie Henson and Cyril Ritchard as two Indian Army Officers in full mess kit. From their vantage point in the stage box they interrupted throughout. In doing so, it became a constant challenge to see if they could make Stanley 'dry' or laugh. As Stanley himself recalls:

> If they had succeeded the sketch would lose all credibility and it was one of the hardest jobs of my life to resist the leg-pulling of that sophisticated artist Cyril Ritchard and my beloved, gravelly voiced, friend Leslie Henson.

The section of musical comedy performances which opens on page 21 represents a further range of Stanley's own work on stage. The first song, 'It'll Be All the Same' was originally performed by Leslie Henson as the finale of 'A Night Out' at the Winter Garden in 1920. Stanley remembers both the song and the artist who first performed it with particular affection, since it was Leslie Henson who gave him his first real West End opportunities. In later years, Stanley adopted the song as an ideal ending to his one-man shows and always enjoyed its cheery fatalism.

'The King who Wanted Jam for Tea' was one of Stanley's most popular songs in 'The Co-Optimists' – the concert party series in which he starred from 1921 to 1927. Like many Co-Optimist songs the words – by the concert-party specialist 'Rex' Newman – had a gentle dig at some facet of the British way of life – in this case, early-closing day.

In 1927, Stanley returned to musical comedy in Vincent Youman's and Irving Caesar's 'Hit the Deck' at the London Hippodrome. Partnered by Ivy Tresmand, Stanley made 'Sometimes I'm Happy' one of the great song standards of the 'twenties. It began a life-long mutual admiration society. For Ivy Tresmand: 'Stanley Holloway is a pet. He gives when you work with him. He's one of the loveliest partners and one of the most generous.' For Stanley, Ivy Tresmand's charms were no less appealing: 'She was a great person, well turned-out, beautifully manicured and she smelt divine!'

'Keep Smiling' marked another return to musical comedy by

Stanley, this time at Drury Lane in 1934. Stanley was, by then, fully embarked on a ten-year spell performing his monologues on the Halls. He could not, however, resist the invitation from Jerome Kern and Oscar Hammerstein to join their new show, 'Three Sisters'. Stanley hoped that they would let him use some of his own monologue material, but Oscar Hammerstein insisted on composing a monologue specially for the occasion. Hence, the rather strange American version of the British monologue – which, in the show, Stanley as Police Constable Eustace Titherley composes for the benefit of his co-star, Albert Burdon.

'Three Sisters' was one of the few Kern/Hammerstein failures and Stanley was soon back on the Halls with his 'Albert' and 'Sam' monologues. He decided that some new musical material was necessary to supplement his Northern recitations. 'My Missus' was a sentimental Cockney ballad with words by Stanley himself. It was set to music by his accompanist Leo Conriche for a performance at the Finsbury Park Empire in 1935.

'Careless Talk' was written by Graham John for Stanley and Leslie Henson as a kind of sophisticated patter act somewhat in the style of the Western Brothers. They first performed it in 1940 at the Saville Theatre in 'Up and Doing' and for the next two years they used this song with constantly changing lyrics which they amended to bring in topical events. These changes were faithfully recorded by Stanley on the inside of a white 'dicky'. Sadly, all this precious material was lost when the Savile Theatre was hit in the London Blitz and the show had to go out on tour.

'Get Me to the Church on Time' and 'Wiv a Little Bit of Luck' need, as they say, virtually no introduction as Stanley's songs in *My Fair Lady*. They were first performed on Broadway at the Mark Hellinger Theatre on 15 March 1956 and were equally successful when the show transferred to the Theatre Royal, Drury Lane on 30 April 1958. What with two-year appearances both in London and on Broadway and the 1964 film version, Stanley has sung these particular songs several thousands of times. 'And yet,' he says 'they are still a constant joy to me. They were both designed to capture the flavour of the music-halls of my youth and they succeeded brilliantly.'

Following *My Fair Lady*, Stanley made many television appearances in the United States. He worked with Maurice Chevalier, Bob Hope and with Groucho Marx on the 'Bell Telephone Hour'. But of all the artists he appeared with on television, Dean Martin stands out as the most humorous, kind and considerate. It was in

'The Dean Martin Show' that Stanley first mastered the brilliant but tricky lyrics of Stephen Sondheim which are reflected in 'Comedy Tonight'.

Stanley decided that, after *My Fair Lady*, he would not appear again in a stage musical. As he puts it: 'For me, it has to be the greatest musical of all time and I wanted to go out of that particular world at the top.' But there was one invitation to appear in a stage musical again which Stanley could not refuse. This was at the Phoenix Theatre on 16 December 1969 when virtually the whole entertainment world gathered to pay tribute to Noël Coward on his seventieth birthday. Stanley, who had in his career sung so many London songs, saluted 'The Master' by singing one of the best: Noël Coward's own 'London Pride'.

If that performance marked the end of Stanley's musical comedy work on stage, happily it led to a new dimension in his long-standing recording career. As the last of the great links with the Victorian and Edwardian Music-Hall, he has been able to give us many impressions of the great performers of his youth. The songs which begin on page 37, are samples of this work which takes us back early into the nineteenth century. As Stanley says:

> In recent years, I've been able to fulfil a long cherished ambition to bring to the notice of the present-day public the songs that were popular 60, 70, even 80 years ago and before that even, before the music-hall when they used to have Saturday night concerts in song and supper rooms like Gatti's and taverns like the Eagle.

In satirical ballards like 'My Lord Tomnoddy' we are able to learn not just about the kind of entertainment our forefathers enjoyed but also of the social values of a time when hanging was regarded as a public pastime. The social niceties of the period are finely observed, even to the description of the 'Tiger Tim' – the footman in splendid livery who, with other footmen, dutifully accompanied his master on the back of his carriage.

'Goin' to the Derby' represents the other end of the social scale with its picture of the costermonger and his little donkey cart on their day off. Costermongers were originally Irish immigrants who left Ireland during the famine of the 1840s, and were rapidly assimilated in Cockney society and slang. Thus their work selling Costard apples was soon termed 'costermongering'. This song based on their annual outing to the Derby was first performed by artists like J. M. Rowley, known as Rowley Over because of his habit of ending his turn by somersaulting up to the footlights.

These first music-hall songs were evocative of the period even before Stanley's birth. But it is difficult to time them precisely. There is no such difficulty with 'The Dark Girl Dress'd in Blue', which was written and sung by Harry Clifton at the London Music-Hall to commemorate the Great Exhibition of 1862. By Clifton's standards this song was positively racey because he was often referred to as a drawing-room vocalist. He usually concentrated on motto songs with a high moral tone such as 'Work Boys, Work and be Contented' and 'Up With the Lark in the Morning'.

'Act on The Square Boys' and 'A Motto for Every Man' are two examples of this type of 'uplift' song. 'Act on the Square Boys' was first sung at the Oxford Music-Hall by The Great Vance in 1866. Vance (born Alfred Peck Stevens) was one of the first of the singers of the 1860s and 1870s who were known as the 'Lion Comiques' ('a Lion of a Comic'). Probably the last of this breed was Arthur Lloyd who was a pioneer of concert party touring entertainment. 'A Motto for Every Man' was one of his most popular numbers.

By contrast with the 'heavy swell' style songs, 'I Live in Trafalgar Square' was typical of the more irreverent strain ushered in by the Edwardian era. It was first sung by Morney Cash in 1902 as a tramp who apes the manners of high society. But it was a woman who was to bring the 'broken down swell' song to its brilliant best when the male impersonator Ella Shields first performed 'Burlington Bertie from Bow' at Newcastle in 1914. The song, written by Ella Shields' husband William Hargreaves, has been performed subsequently by many male impersonators but, for timing and the ultimate 'la-di-da' parody, it is difficult to imagine a better version than Stanley's own recording in 1964, especially when the tramp describes the bloodstock sales at Kempton Park:

> I lean on some awning
> While Lord Derby's yawning
> And he bids two thousand
> And I bid – Good Morning.

William Hargreaves not only wrote songs for his wife but also for many of the other performers whom Stanley was later to recall as representing widely different types of comedian. One such was Billy Williams – billed as 'The Man in the Velvet Suit'. He was one of the first clean-faced comics and carried a large handkerchief into which he would laugh until he wept. He used this to great effect when he left the stage at the end of 'Oh, I Must Go Home Tonight!' written in 1908. Apart from this example of the laughing comedian's work, the song is also interesting as an obvious forerunner of 'I'm Getting Married in the Morning'.

'I Thowt Mebbe I Would – An' I Did' and 'I Went Down to Bright' were the work of two more of Stanley's great music-hall favourites. Jack Pleasants, the shy Yorkshire comedian, was billed as 'The Bashful Linit' when he performed 'I Thowt Mebbe I Would'. He worked in strong North Country dialogue but Stanley's recorded impression of this performer was noticeable for the way he sang very softly to convey shyness but ended with a final giggle on 'An' I Did'.

'I Went Down to Bright,' as the text shows, is a rare example of the work of the abbreviating comic. It is doubtful if the original material was ever published and it is recalled for us by Stanley as performed by Phil Ray with whom he appeared at the Tivoli in 1912. Stanley recalls that he was so blind that his dresser had to wait in the wings to put on his glasses. He had a nice line in throwaway gags such as: 'I remember that day particularly because I was coming out of a pub. Well, you must come out sometimes for meals and to get some more money!'

'Champagne Charlie' was re-written in 1944 by Ernest Irving and Frank Eyton for the film of the same name which was based on the rivalry between George Leybourne and The Great Vance. Stanley played Vance who had sung 'Cliquot, Cliquot, That's the Wine for Me' at the Oxford while Tommy Trinder as Leybourne replied at the Canterbury with 'Champagne Charlie' (which Leybourne had written with Albert Lee in 1886). Between times, the two great 'Lion Comiques' traded a wide range of drinking songs from 'Cool Burgundy Ben' and 'John Barleycorn' to 'Burgundy, Claret and Port (That's My Favourite Sport)'.

Stanley's appearance in this wartime film was part of a new work pattern which kept him off the stage for almost ten years. In that time he made over thirty-three film appearances. As the public became increasingly aware of his wide range of acting skills, it was no surprise when his recording work became similarly varied. Full-scale Shakespeare productions for Caedmon Records Limited led to the never-never-land where singing and literature came together as comic recitation. The samples of Edward Lear and W. S. Gilbert's verse which begin on page 63 are no more than a smattering of an enormous recorded output which has kept Stanley hard at work for most of the last twenty years.

Over the same period he has still been busy with stage, film and television appearances. 1 October 1980 marks Stanley's ninetieth birthday and there is no other performer who can match his activity over the entire entertainment spectrum, from his debut as a boy soprano in 1900 until the present day. Earlier this year, BBC Radio 2 marked Stanley's ninetieth year in a six-part life story. Working with Stanley on that series and on the monologue and song books has been a great experience. To hear at first hand of so many entertainment giants of the past is thrilling – especially when the raconteur speaks as the most versatile performer of our time.

But what gives it such special delight is to find a man in his ninetieth year so full of life, with an enormous sense of humour and an overwhelming modesty. 'Well, I suppose I've got from nothing to something', is the most he allows himself. So it is fitting that Stanley's final song is one which he chose for this work as a postscript. It is clearly one with which he identifies himself – Old Barty, who has also achieved 'four score and ten' and who is 'well known round here'.

To Stanley Holloway and his devoted wife, Laney, this book is a small present to mark his ninetieth year. Long may they continue to enjoy the happy memories it contains for all of us.

MICHAEL MARSHALL
May 1980

NOTES AND ACKNOWLEDGEMENTS

The thirty-three monologues and songs in this book are designed to give a flavour of Stanley Holloway's work in virtually every field of entertainment.

The dates of the monologues shown in Part I are the years in which material was originally composed. The dates of the musical comedy performances in Part II and the humorous poetry in Part IV are the years in which Stanley Holloway first performed the items in question. The dates shown for music-hall performers in Part III are the years (where known) of the first performance of each item by their original artists. Details of Stanley Holloway's own recording dates are given in the Discography on pages 75–7.

In compiling this material, much of which has never previously been published, I am indebted to Steve Allen, Chris Morgan, Alan Owen and Derek Bromberg of the BBC for their help in tracing rare recorded material. I am also grateful to my secretary, Anne Buckingham, and Patrick Howgill of EMI for their work in transcribing recordings. Once again, I have been greatly helped by Roger Houghton and Felicity Astley-Cooper at Elm Tree Books, and, finally, as ever, my thanks to my wife Caroline for her forbearance.

The author and publishers would also like to thank the following for their kind permission to reproduce copyright material in this book: Chappell & Co. Ltd for *Sometimes I'm Happy* © 1927 by Harms Inc.; *Keep Smiling* © 1934 by Jerome Kern; *Get Me to the Church on Time* © 1956 by Alan Jay Lerner & Frederick Loewe; *Wiv a Little Bit of Luck* © 1956 by Alan Jay Lerner & Frederick Loewe; *Comedy Tonight* © 1962 by Stephen Sondheim; *I Thowt Mebbe I Would – An' I Did* © 1922 by Chappell & Co. Ltd. Francis Day & Hunter for *And Yet I Don't Know!* © 1922; *'My Word! You Do Look Queer!'* © 1923; *I Live in Trafalgar Square* ©

xvi

1902; *The King who Wanted Jam for Tea* © 1925. EMI Music Publishing Ltd for *George Lashwood Monologue* © 1942 by Frank Eyton; *My Missus* © 1935 by Stanley Holloway; *Careless Talk* © 1960 by Stanley Holloway & Leslie Henson; *I Went Down to Bright* © 1912 by Phil Ray. Reynolds Music Ltd for *The Street Watchman's Story* © *1910; On Strike* © 1906; *Evings' Dorg 'Ospital* © 1906; *Pukka Sahib* © 1940. B. Feldman & Co. for *It'll Be All the Same* © 1920 by Herman Darewski; *Oh, I Must Go Home Tonight!* © 1908; *Champagne Charlie* © 1944. Dr Jan Van Loewen Ltd for *London Pride* © 1941 by Chappell & Co. Ltd. Lawrence Wright Music Co. Ltd for *Burlington Bertie from Bow* © 1915. Boosey & Hawkes Music Publishers Ltd for *Old Barty* © 1919.

PART I

Monologues

AND YET I DON'T KNOW!
(Buying a Wedding Present)
by R. P. Weston and Bert Lee (1919)

Now, my sister's daughter Elizabeth May
Is going to get married next Sunday, they say.
Now, what shall I buy her? She's such a nice gel!
I think a piano would do very well.
I saw one today, only ninety-five pound:
A decent piano, I'll have it sent round.

And yet I don't know! And yet I don't know!
I think she's the rottenest player I know.
And if she keeps thumping out that 'Maiden's Pray'r'
The husband might kill his young bride, and so there!
I won't buy the piano! It's not that I'm mean;
I think I'd best buy her a sewing machine.

And yet I don't know! And yet I don't know!
A sewing machine is a 'tenner' or so!
A 'tenner' would buy lots of needles and thread,
And things that are hand-made are best, so it's said.
So it's not that I'm mingey, although I'm half Scotch –
I know what I'll buy her; an Ingersoll watch!

And yet I don't know! And yet I don't know!
In five or six years they're too fast or too slow.

1

And when she's turn'd seventy, that's if she's spar'd,
'Twill have cost her a fortune in being repair'd.
Or else she'll have pawn'd it, and lost it, so there!
I know what I'll buy her; a jumper to wear!

And yet I don't know! And yet I don't know!
The girls won't wear jumpers in ten years or so.
Besides she might start getting fat before long.
And fat girls in jumpers show too much ong bong!
And open work jumpers give ladies the 'flu,
I'll buy her some handkerchiefs; that's what I'll do!

And yet I don't know! And yet I don't know!
Good hankies cost twelve bob a dozen or so.
And twelve bob's too much for her poor Uncle John.
Why, anything does just to blow your nose on.
And talking of noses, hers looks red enough!
I know what I'll buy her; a nice powder puff.

She can't powder her nose with a grand piano,
Nor yet with a sewing machine.
She can't powder her nose with an Ingersoll watch:
Well, it's silly! You see what I mean!

She can't powder her nose with a jumper:
She would find it a little bit rough;
So I'll go round to Woolworth's tonight, God bless her!
And buy her a powder puff.

And yet I don't know! And yet I don't know!
Sixpence ha'p'nies don't grow in backyards,
So I don't think I'll send her a powder puff,
I'll send her – my kindest regards!

'MY WORD! YOU DO LOOK QUEER!'
by R. P. Weston and Bert Lee (1923)

I've been very poorly but now I feel prime,
I've been out today for the very first time.
I felt like a lad as I walk'd down the road,
Then I met old Jones and he said, 'Well, I'm blow'd!'

'My word you do look queer! My word you do look queer!
Oh, dear! You look dreadful; you've had a near shave,
You look like a man with one foot in the grave.'
I said, 'Bosh! I'm better; it's true I've been ill.'
He said, 'I'm delighted you're better, but still,
I wish you'd a thousand for me in your will.
My word, you do look queer!'

That didn't improve me, it quite put me back,
Still, I walk'd farther on, and I met Cousin Jack.
He look'd at me hard and he murmur'd, 'Gee whiz!
It's like him! It can't be! It isn't! It is!
By gosh! Who'd have thought it? Well, well, I declare!
I'd never have known you except for your hair.

'My word you do look queer! My word you do look queer!
Your cheeks are all sunk and your colour's all gone,
Your neck's very scraggy, still you're getting on.
How old are you now? About fifty, that's true.
Your father died that age, your mother did too.
Well, the black clothes I wore then'll come in for you.
My word! You do look queer!'

That really upset me; I felt quite cast down,
But I tried to buck up, and then up came old Brown.
He star'd at me hard, then he solemnly said,
'You shouldn't be out, you should be home in bed.
I heard you were bad, well I heard you were gone.
You look like a corpse with an overcoat on.

'My word you do look queer! My word you do look queer!
You'd best have a brandy before you drop dead.'
So, pale as a sheet I crawl'd in the 'King's Head'.
The bar-maid sobbed, 'Oh you poor fellow,' and then
She said, 'On the slate you owe just one-pound-ten.
You'd better pay up, we shan't see you again.
My word you do look queer!'

My knees started knocking, I did feel so sad.
Then Brown said, 'Don't die in a pub, it looks bad!'
He said, 'Come with me, I'll show you what to do.
Now I've got a friend who'll be useful to you.'
He led me to Black's Undertaking Depot,
And Black, with some crepe round his hat said, 'Hello,

'My word you do look queer! My word you do look queer!
Now we'll fix you up for a trifling amount.
Now what do you say to a bit on account?'
I said, 'I'm not dying.' He said, 'Don't say that!
My business of late has been terribly flat,
But I'm telling my wife she can have that new hat.
My word you do look queer!'

I crawl'd in the street and I murmur'd, 'I'm done.'
Then up came old Jenkins and shouted, 'Old son!'
'My word you do look well! My word you do look well!
You're looking fine and in the pink!'
I shouted, 'Am I? Come and have a drink!
You've put new life in me, I'm sounder than a bell.
By gad! There's life in the old dog yet.
My word I do feel well!'

THE STREET WATCHMAN'S STORY
by Charles J. Winter (1910)

Some chaps gets the fat, and some chaps gets the lean,
When they start on their journey thro' life,
Some makes pots of money by being M.P.s
And some gets it by taking a wife.
Some learns a good trade such as Dustman or Sweep,
Which the same I'd have done if I'd knowed,
But the special profession I've drifted to now
Is 'Minding a 'ole in the road'.
As a rule it's a nice quiet comfortable job,
But there's times when I've hated the work,
For instance I once had to go Christmas Day
On a job which I'd tried hard to shirk.
I minded that 'ole, sir, the whole blessed day,
Till my dinner and teatime had gone,
And my Christmas dinner (if any was left)
I should have when relieved later on.
At home we'd some friends and we'd got a big goose,
And I'd ordered a half ton of coal,
Yet here was I sitting at seven P. hem
A-shivering in front o' my 'ole.
And I thought of them all making merry at home,
Stuffed with goose from their heads to their toes,
They'd just about leave me a cut off the beak,
Or the end of the Parson's nose.
And I sat quite despondent and dozed half asleep,
I was feeling quite humpy and sore,
When from one of the big houses just on my right
A swell flunkey stepped out through the door.
He came straight to me and he said with a bow,
Which made his gold lace gleam and shine,
'The Countess's compliments as you're alone
She'll be pleased if you'll step in and dine.'
Well I very near dropped to the ground with surprise,
For it wasn't a safe thing to do.

7

What if thieves came and pinched a great heap of them stones,
Or 'opped off with a drain-pipe or two?
Then I thought of the Countess's kindness of 'eart
How she'd thought of me lonely outside,
So I scraped the clay off my boots with a spade
And I follered the flunkey inside.
And there sat the Countess all merry and bright
With diamonds and jewels all a-glow.
In a silk dress which must have cost nigh twenty pound,
Though there wasn't much of it you know.
Her husband the Viscount was there at her side,
While the waiters flew round with a whizz,
And in half a jiff I was seated with them
A-eating and shifting the fizz.
The Viscount he drank to my jolly good health
As he took from his wine-glass a pull,
I only just nodded – I couldn't say much –
For my mouth, like my heart, was too full.
When we'd finished, us gents all puts on a cigar,
And the perfume was simply sublime,
By the bands that was on 'em, why I'll guarantee
They must have cost fourpence a time.
Then the ladies they starts playing 'Kiss-in-the-ring'
And the Countess enjoyed the game too,
When she gets in the ring she just turns straight to me
And she says, 'Mr Nobbs, I'll have you.'
O, I didn't know which was my 'ead or my 'eels,
It was like being in Fai-ry-land,
But I threw down my smoke and I wiped my moustache,
Just like this, with the back of my 'and.
She put up her lips looking saucy and sweet,
And I blush'd as towards her I stole,
I bent forward and then I woke up just in time,
Or I might have fell clean down the 'ole.

ON STRIKE
by Charles Pond (1906)

When I lays dahn my tools I lays 'em dahn,
I laid 'em dahn seven year ago over a matter of three shilling a
    week.
Now there's people 'oo'll say 'Fancy a man being aht o' work
    seven year over a matter o'three shilling a week.'
People what don't understand the principle of the thing,
The principle of a fair living wage and that's wot I'm a-standin'
    aht for.
And I wouldn't let my old woman work for the money she do in
    the steam laundry,
Only somebody's got to keep the 'ome up.
It would never do for both ov us to be aht.
She was only a-sayin' to me the other morning as she was a-
    bringing me up my cup o' tea and a bit o' toast afore she was
    goin' aht t' work,
'Why don't you get into Parliament?'
And that's where I ought t' be.
And the first Act o' Parliament I should pass 'd be
Concerning the hover-crowdin' on the hearly mornin'
    trams.
A woman can't git t' 'er work, she's got t' walk and walk 'ome
    again.
Now you know there's 'eaps o' fings want haltering in this 'ere
    country,
But you'll never get nuthin' done so long as they won't fink.
Fink! Why, they won't even read.
Why you can see 'undreds and fahsands goin' out t' work wivaht
    even 'avin' read their mornin' paper.
Why you know the most terrible fings might 'appen during th'
    night,
The most frightful disaster, the most 'orrible national
    castostrophe.
Why Bass's Brewery might be burnt t' the grahnd
And a man'd start work in a state of blind hignorance.

Now I remember th' time when there was 'a interest took in politics,

I remember the time at hour political club when you couldn't get near the bar on a Sunday morning.

And wot do yer find nah? A few bicycles outside and 'arf the trade in the place small lemons.

And that's wot old England's a-driftin' to.

Now the Chancellor of the Hexchequer said the other day,

'E says – and I quite agree wiv 'im fer once,

'E says the falling off in the consumption of beer is halarming.

The falling off in the consumption of beer *is* halarming.

But there's something more halarming what the Chancellor of the Hexchequer did not tell you,

And that is this,

That concurrently simultaneous and identical wiv the fallin' off in the consumption of beer

Is the total and utter disappearance of the conversational powers of man.

For I defy anyone to get hup a political hargument on cocoa.

It can't be done.

Now I'm a paper-'anger be trade I am and wild 'orses can't drag me from paper-'anging,

The very last time I picked hup my tools seven year ago

They tried it on wiv me but it didn't come orf,

They didn't know 'oo they was a-dealin' wiv.

I got the money what I arsked afore I started on me job which was the stripping of a wall.

Well, I 'adn't been a-workin' for a couple of hours before I comes across an old bell wire in the wall.

I called up the foreman. 'What's the matter wiv you?' 'e says.

I says, 'Look at this old bell wire in the wall.'

'Pull it aht,' 'e says. 'What?' I says.

'Pull it aht,' 'e says.

I says, 'You'll pardon me, that's plumber's work.' And I lays down me tools.

And when I lays dahn me tools, I lays 'em dahn.

EVINGS' DORG 'OSPITAL
by Charles Pond (1906)

'Ere, Evings wasn't always in th' dorg trade,
But wot'd it matter?
Anything that Evings turns 'is 'and to 'e'd make a do of it.
It ain't buyin' or sellin' dorgs what Evings does so well at neither,
It's th' 'ospital under th' shop where Evings gets th' brass.
Five an' twenty t' thirty dorgs at seven an' six a week,
It soon mounts up yer know, and no aht-goin's.
They git nuffin t' eat at Evings's. That's Evings' big secret.
Th' other mornin' Evings was standin' at the door of 'is shop
Scalin' a bull dorg's teef,
When up drives a carridge an' pair
And aht a lady gets with a little Italian grey'ound
Which was snarlin' an' snappin' somethin' shockin'.
Wallop! goes the bulldog dahn the flap into th' 'ospital.
The lady 'ands 'er dorg t' Evings.
'Mind 'e don't bite,' she sez.
'Little dorgs never bite me, Mum,' sez Evings.
Well, I dunno what it is about Evings,
But directly 'e gets 'old of a dorg th' dorg seems t' know somethin'
And never takes 'is eyes orf Evings.
'Is pahr over animals is marv'llous.
Well, look wot 'e's dun wiv Missus Evings.
'Wot's th' matter with th' little feller?' sez Evings.
The lady explained as 'ow 'e used t' be able t' eat steak
But lately only a very tiny bit of chicken nah and agin.
'Poor little dear,' sez Evings.
'But wot's the little chappie's name, Mum?'
'Fido,' sez the lady.
''Ere 'e'll soon be orlright wiv us, Mum,
That is, if 'e aint gone too fur,' sez Evings.
'Seven 'n' six a week is our usual charge
But if 'e 'as been in th' 'abit of eatin' chickin . . .'
Well, the lady offer'd t' make it arf a sov'rin a week
And sez, 'You will be kind to 'im, won't you?'

'Kind t' 'im? Bless you, Mum,' sez Evings,
'D'you know th' 'ard part of this business is partin' with th' little
creatures
At th' end of th' week when their time's up?'
The lady 'ands Evings two luvley cushi'ns,
One for th' day and one for th' night,
And after a lot of kissin' and cuddlin' the carridge drives orf.
Wallop! goes Fido dahn th' flap into th' 'ospital.
'E gets put on a couple of inches of chain
And a combin' and brushin' wot 'e never fergits.
And in less than a couple of days 'e's dartin' abaht
And catchin' the little bits of tripe wot they fling rahnd
As quick as any of 'em.
It was a sight to see 'em as Evings goes dahn wiv th' basket,
All their teeth a-glistenin' and their little rudders a-goin' like
mad.
'E don't 'arf fling it t' 'em and they're on it ev'ry time,
Just abaht 'arf ahnce a-piece.
But it's when the ladies call for th' dorgs as you ought to 'ear
Evings.
When the lady calls for Fido 'e sez, " 'E's orlright nah, Mum,
But we've 'ad a very anxious time wiv th' little feller.
Me and th' Missus was up th' 'ole of th' first night wiv 'im.
I got a little rest th' second night, but th' Missus she stuck to 'im,
And with th' aid of gentle nursin' and 'is own brave little 'eart
We pulled 'im rahnd.'
And 'e goes t' th' flap and 'e sez, 'Bring little Fido up.'
As soon as 'e sees 'is Missus 'e goes nearly mad,
Right over 'er shoulder, aht into th' street,
Up on to th' coachman's box, dahn agin and back into th' shop.
Th' lady was delighted. 'Oh aint 'e improved,' th' lady said.
'Yes, Mum' sez Evings. 'I think when you gets 'im 'ome
You'll find as 'ow 'e'll be able t' eat a little bit of chickin nah.'
The lady 'ands Evings th' sov'rin.
O'course Evings aint got no change, but 'e'd send for it if the lady
wished it.
But the lady wouldn't 'ear of such a thing,
And said she'd be quite sure t' send Mrs Evings a present for 'er
great kindness.
Which Evings sez they didn't expect but would be only too
pleased t' 'ave,
If it was only aht of remb'rance of little Fido

12

'Oo'd endeared 'isself to th' 'earts of all.
Yeh, and there's many a party wouldn't be nearly so snappish
If they 'ad a week at Evings.
But 'e dursn't trust them.
Dorgs can't talk.

THE GEORGE LASHWOOD MONOLOGUE
(From *Fine and Dandy*)
by Frank Eyton (1942)

I've always been a gambler
Since the day when I was born,
And thus you see me standing here
A thing of shame and scorn.
At five years old I stole a shilling
From my Aunt Maria,
And lost it playing pitch and toss
With bad boys in the choir.
I went to Harrow College
While a boy still in me teens,
And got in with the gambling set
And staked beyond me means.
I couldn't pay me card debts
Which was quite a large amount,
And got sneaked on – to the teacher
By the winner – a Viscount.
I got the sack from Harrow
And I had to take the knock,
The scandal made me poor old dad's grey hair
Turn white with shock.
For months I didn't gamble,
Got a job and earned me pay,
And gradually me poor old dad's white hair

Turned back from white to grey.
But I've got the gambling fever
Deeply rooted in me blood,
And having no cards up me sleeve
Was soon dragged in the mud.
One night I lost a cool thou'
And I staggered out a wreck,
And forged another person's name
On someone else's cheque.
The Police, of course, arrested me
For this diabolical crime,
And so it was me dad's grey hair
Turned white a second time.
But now I've served me sentence
And they've set me free again,
So as I'm out of prison
I will sing you this refrain:

I'm going away
I'm going away
I'm leaving my homeland's shore.
I'm going away
I'm going away
An exile from England's door.
I've been a fool
Poker and pool
Have landed me in the cart,
Then a forced bill of sale
Landed me up in jail
And I've broken me parents' hearts.
That's why I'm . . .
Sailing away to Australia
Across all the land, sea and foam,
I've been rather a failure
But I'll start again out there.
Now when I make good in Australia
And find wealth across the foam,
I shall come back from there
And they'll make me Lord Mayor
For the sake of the old folks at home.

PUKKA SAHIB
(Based on *The Green Eye of The Little Yellow God*
by Milton Hayes)
Sketch by Reginald Purdell (1940)

Played in 'Up and Doing' at the Saville Theatre, London,
1940–42, with the following cast of Characters:

The Reciter .... Stanley Holloway
The Colonel .... Leslie Henson
The Major .... Cyril Ritchard

(The Reciter *walks on to the stage and prepares to recite.*)

Reciter: The Green Eye of the little Yellow God, by
                Milton Hayes.
                There's a green-eyed yellow idol to the north of
                Khatmandu
                There's a little marble cross below the town;
                There's a . . .
The Colonel: (*Interrupting from a box.*) Have you been there
                lately?
Reciter: I beg your pardon.
The Major: (*From the box.*) The Colonel said 'Have you been
                there lately?'
Reciter: Where?
Both: Khatmandu.
Reciter: No, as a matter of fact I haven't been there for
                some time.
The Major: What were you there with? Indian Army?
                Indian Civil?
The Colonel: Or the Fol-de-Rols?
Reciter: Well, to be perfectly frank –
The Major: As a matter of fact I know Khatmandu well. It's
                a second home to me.
The Colonel: I love every inch of the place. I was only there
                last year.
The Major: I came through a couple of months ago on my
                way home. The whole place was changed ter-
                ribly.

15

The Colonel:	Yes, bad show.
Reciter:	That's very interesting. But why are you telling me all this.
The Major:	Just to put you right geographically.
The Colonel:	You see, the whole place has been changed under a town planning scheme.
The Major:	For instance, there's a large public library and public baths combined erected in the square. The Office of Works have moved the idol to the south of Khatmandu.
The Colonel:	And the cemetery has been moved and there is now a cinema. Hideous thing.
The Major:	So that marble cross you spoke about is now above the town.
Reciter:	Perhaps I'd better start again.
Both:	But do.
Reciter:	The Green Eye of the Little Yellow God, by Milton Hayes. There's a green-eyed yellow idol to the . . .
The Major:	South.
Reciter:	South of Khatmandu. There's a little marble cross . . .
The Colonel:	Above.
Reciter:	(*Dully.*) Above the town. There's a broken-hearted woman tends the grave of Mad Carew.
The Major:	Did you know Fanny Shannon?
Reciter:	Did I know who?
The Major:	Fanny Shannon. You remember General Shannon's eldest girl.
The Colonel:	Tim Shannon – damn good scout.
The Major:	Yes indeed, You're quite out of order saying she's broken-hearted. She was naturally upset at Carew's death, but she got over it.
The Colonel:	Didn't she marry a rich American?
The Major:	Yes, they've got three boys at St Paul's.
Reciter:	How then shall I describe her?
The Major:	Oh – (*Whispers to the Colonel.*) We suggest a comparatively broken-hearted woman.
Reciter:	I'd better start again.
Both:	But do.
The Major:	Only you don't mind if we have a drink.

The Colonel:	Splendid idea. (*He rises to go.*)
The Major:	Oh, there's no need to go, Colonel. You can get one here. I've got Sabu standing by. (*An Indian Servant enters and salutes.*)
The Major:	What will you have?
The Colonel:	I'll have a chota-peg.
The Major:	One chota-peg, and I'll have a Passion Fruit. (*The Indian Servant exits.*) Oh, and Sabu – not too much fruit.
Reciter:	May I carry on?
Both:	But do.
Reciter:	There's a green-eyed yellow idol to the South of Khatmandu. There's a little marble cross above the town. There's a comparatively broken-hearted woman Tends the grave of Mad Carew and the little god for ever gazes down.
The Colonel:	Up, sir, up.
Reciter:	(*Hastily.*) Up. He was known as Mad Carew.
The Major:	Oh, ridiculous. The man wasn't mad at all, he was mentally deficient yes. You couldn't call him absolutely crackers.
Reciter:	He was known as mentally deficient Carew by the Subs. of Khatmandu. He was hotter than they felt inclined to tell.
The Colonel:	Too much curry powder. Too much Mepharine.
Reciter:	(*Miserably.*) But for all his foolish pranks ...
The Major:	Foolish pranks be damned, sir. You don't call writing rude words on the walls foolish pranks.
Reciter:	Well, I didn't know.
The Colonel:	No, neither did I.
The Major:	What, Carew? Horrible habits.
The Colonel:	Tell me a couple. (*They whisper.*) No – Government House.
The Major:	Government House. I tell you, the Viceroy was livid. In front of Noël Coward, too.
Reciter:	He was worshipped in the ranks. And the Colonel's daughter smiled on him as well ... (*The Colonel and the Major rise.*)
The Major:	Now, that's a cad's remark, sir. If you want to

	know, my brother was engaged to her at the time.
	I . . . (*He attempts to climb over the box.*)
Reciter:	I'm sorry, I didn't know. I apologise.
The Colonel:	I should darn well think so. (*To the Major.*) I'd accept his apology.
The Major:	Would you? Very well, we don't want a scene.
The Colonel:	We needn't look.
The Major:	No, turn your back on the blighter. (*He picks up a programme.*) Who is he? (*Announces Reciter's name.*) Never heard of him. Hippodrome or local theatre, I suppose.
Reciter:	She was nearly twenty-one.
The Colonel:	(*With a roar of derisive laughter.*) Twenty-one be damned! She was thirty-nine if she was a day.
The Major:	Mind you, she didn't look it. She had everything lifted – or practically everything. All the main essentials.
Reciter:	And arrangements had been made to celebrate her birthday with a ball.
The Colonel:	Extraordinary. I don't remember that.
The Major:	No, I think you were away at the time. It was during the rains. You were up at Rumblechelly-pore – on that sewage commission.
Reciter	He wrote to ask what present she would like from Mentally Deficient Carew. They met next day as he dismissed his squad.
The Colonel:	Platoon.
Reciter:	As he dismissed his squad.
The Colonel:	Platoon.
Reciter:	Squad.
The Colonel:	The Subaltern commands a platoon.
Reciter:	But it must be a squad, it's got to rhyme with yellow God.
The Major:	We don't give a hoot what it's got to rhyme with, sir. King's Regulations – it's a platoon.
Reciter:	They met next day as he dismissed his platoon. And jokingly she said that nothing else would do But the green eye of the . . .
The Major:	Chocolate-coloured coon . . .
The Colonel:	(*Roaring with laughter.*) Jolly good.

Reciter:	(*Hysterically.*) The night before the dance. Mentally Deficient Carew sat in a trance.
The Major:	Sat in a trance – he sat in a blancmange. I remember it well. He was as tight as a tick.
Reciter:	And they chafed him as they puffed at their cigars.
The Colonel:	Wait a minute. Chafed him? Are you referring to his underwear or his brother officers?
Reciter:	His brother officers.
The Major:	Then the word is chaffed – or if you come from the North Country – the 'A' is short and it would be chaft.
Reciter:	It might interest you to know that I do come from the North Country. I would prefer the word chaft.
The Colonel:	Then by all means say chaft.
Reciter:	Very well, I will say chaft.
Both:	But do.
Reciter:	(*Lapsing into North Country.*) And they chaft him as they puffed at their cigars.

(*The Colonel and the Major laugh and applaud.*)

(*Enter the Indian Servant. He speaks in double-talk Hindustani.*)

The Major:	Oh, we can't get a drink here. Come on, let's go to the bar. Sorry we've got to go, so we'll leave you poofing and chaffing.
Reciter:	Gentlemen, please, Gentlemen, will you please let me continue. Don't you realize this is my livelihood, my business? May I please continue?
Both:	But do. (*They both laugh.*)
Reciter:	(*Going mad.*) There's a broken-hearted Idol To the West of Mad Carew; There's a cross-eyed yellow woman Doing all a Cat Can Doo. Ha Ha Ha!

(*He screams insanely and rushes from the stage.*)

PART II

Musical Comedy Performances

IT'LL BE ALL THE SAME
(A Hundred Years from Now)
by Arthur Anderson (1920)

I've been fairly on my beam-ends,
For a long, long time.
When your childhood's happy dream ends,
Life's a weary up-hill climb.
Though I'm never on the right side,
Somehow I blunder through;
I keep looking on the bright side,
It's the only thing to do.

Refrain
It'll be all the same, just the same
A hundred years from now;
No use a-worrying,
No use a-flurrying,
No use kicking up a row.
I shan't be here,
You won't be here,
When the hundred years are gone,
But somebody else will be well in the cart,
And the world will still go on!

Take your troubles as you find them,
And they soon take wing!

21

Let folks think you do not mind them,
And they almost lose their sting!
Fate is ever waiting for you,
No matter why, or when,
Maybe, someday, she will floor you,
Even if she does, what then?

Refrain
It'll be all the same, just the same
A hundred years from now;
No use a-worrying,
No use a-flurrying,
No use kicking up a row.
I shan't be here,
You won't be here,
When the hundred years are gone,
But somebody else will be well in the cart,
And the world will still go on!

THE KING WHO WANTED JAM FOR TEA
by Greatrex Newman (1925)

There was a King of high degree, who lived in Timbuctoo,
He had a noble pedigree, his blood was bluest blue.
His life was spent in sweet content, from care and worry free.
But one day to his Queen he said, 'I'm tired of butter on my
    bread,
So as a little change instead, I'd like some jam for tea.'

The Queen she hung her pretty head and turning to her spouse,
She said, 'I'm sorry, dear, there's no jam in the house.
I meant to get a pot when up in town,' she said,
'So would you like a little slice of currant cake instead?
We've got no jam or even marmalade,
So try a little slice of cake, it's all home-made.'

The King he gave a sulky frown, his eye with anger shone,
Then reached his overcoat and crown and quickly put them on.
He took his new umbrella too and went out with a slam,
Then hurried down the busy street, with carpet slippers on his
    feet,
To give himself a special treat, and buy a pot of jam.

As he got near the grocer's shop he smiled with joyful glee,
He thought, 'With bread and jam, I'll have a scrumptious tea.'
But when he reached the grocer's door it filled him with dismay,
The shutters wide, were up outside,
'Twas early closing day!
'Twas early closing day!
'Twas early closing day!

The King said 'Bother' and 'Tut tut', then in a temper flew,
Then cried because the shop was shut, for what was he to do?
His handkerchief was wet with grief, and with a sob said he,
'My crown into the sea I'll fling, The "Red Flag" I will learn to
    sing,
For what's the use of being a King,
If you can't have jam for tea?
Oh what's the use of being a King,
If you can't have jam for tea?
Oh what's the use of being a King,
If you can't have jam for tea?
My crown into the sea I'll fling,
For what's the use of being a King,
If you can't have jam for tea?'

SOMETIMES I'M HAPPY
Performed by Stanley Holloway and Ivy Tresmand in 'Hit the
Desk' (1927)
by Irving Caesar and Vincent Thomas

S.H.   Ev'ry day seems like a year,
I.T.   Sweetheart, when you are not near.
S.H.   All that you claim must be true
I.T.   For I'm just the same as you.

S.H.	Sometimes I'm happy,
	Sometimes I'm blue,
	My disposition depends on you.
	I never mind the rain from the skies,
	If I can find the sun in your eyes.
	Sometimes I love you,
	Sometimes I hate you;
	But when I hate you,
	It's 'cause I love you.
	That's how I am, so what can I do?
	I'm happy when I'm with you!

S.H.	Stars are smiling at me from your eyes.
I.T.	Sunbeams now there will be in the skies.
S.H.	Tell me that you will be true!
I.T.	That will all depend on you, dear!

I.T.	Sometimes I'm happy,
	Sometimes I'm blue,
	My disposition depends on you.
	I never mind the rain from the skies,
	If I can find the sun in your eyes.

Unison	Sometimes I love you,
	Sometimes I hate you;
	But when I hate you,
	It's 'cause I love you,
	That's how I am, so what can I do?
	I'm happy when I'm with you!

24

KEEP SMILING

Performed by Stanley Holloway and Albert Burdon in
'Three Sisters' (1934)
by Oscar Hammerstein

A.B.   Hullo, Eustace. Written any good songs lately?

S.H.   Yes, I've just finished one.

A.B.   Do you find it difficult to do?

S.H.   Yeah, but I find you can learn the words easier when
you write 'em yourself.

A.B.   What sort of a song is it?

S.H.   Well it's a serious sort of song, you know. Makes you
stop and think. I'll sing it for yer:

> A child of only three
> Sat on his father's knee,
> The sun was shining brightly from above
> The child of three said, 'Dad,
> To have you I am glad;
> But why do I never have
> A mother's love?'
> At first the father coughed,
> To hide the way he felt.

A.B.   'Ere, 'ere. Wait a minute. Would you mind repeating
that.

S.H.   At first the father coughed,
To hide the way he felt.

A.B.   Yeah, that's what I thought you said. Carry on.

S.H.   At first the father coughed
To hide the way he felt
And then he said, 'My child,
It's time you knew.
I have a tale to tell,
And I will tell it well,
But first I'd like to sing you this refrain:

> Keep smiling,
> Remember you're a man.
> Laugh away your care,
> That's the only plan.
> Keep smiling,

And always wear a grin,
That's the spirit that I think
Will sometimes win.

I never shall forget
The day when first we met;
I asked her and she said
That she'd be mine.
And then I took her home
And showed her to me mother;
And then I took a walk
While they made friends
On the road to Mandalay
Where the village smithy lay.

A.B.   'Ere, 'ere, 'ere.
S.H.   Yes, I know, I got that wrong.
        That's another song altogether.
A.B.   You didn't write that one.
S.H.   No, that's one by Robert Burns.

. . . And then I took a walk
While they made friends.
That summer we were wed
I kissed her on the head
And then we lived happily in a little red house and
Had three children then
Her father died and I lost me job but
Years later we got a cable from
Mesopotamia – they'd struck oil on me
Uncle's property and we'd come into
Practically thirty thousand pounds.

Yes, I know. I've got to get those last few lines
polished up a bit. Yes, I've got to get the words fitted
in better. But still:

Keep smiling,
Remember you're a man,
Laugh away your care,
That's the only plan.
Keep smiling,
And always wear a grin,
That's the spirit that I think
Will sometimes win . . .

MY MISSUS
by Stanley Holloway (1935)

Ah! Charlie Brahn's the name folks, and I'm aht upon th' spree.
'Cos Why? because today's me weddin' anniversary.
You'd like to meet the Missus,
But she can't get away,
She's workin' late tonight 'cos it's the other girl's arf day.
Nah, you wouldn't call 'er tall,
In fact, she's rather small,
But 'er 'eart is so much bigger than 'er brain.
And still I'm bahnd t' say, she's just th' same t'day
As when in Church she took my name.
O' course we 'as our ups and dahns like other people do,
And little scraps when we don't quite agree.
And if yer'd like t'meet 'er,
I'll be prahd to introduce,
My Missus Brahn wot's known as Missus B.

We never 'ad no kids,
We lives all upon our own.
We rubs along tergether,
I'm 'er Derby, she's my Joan.
And th' place where we reside
Well, it's nothin' posh or smart,
It's dahn in Camden Tahn and we've just got th' hupper part.
But still I'm bahnd t' say, she's just th' same t'day
As when in Church she took my name.
And when she reaches up above,
When 'er life's work is done,
And at th' gate where Peter 'olds th' key
She gives 'er name,
'E'll say 'Come in,
We kept a special place
For Missus Brahn wot's known as Missus B.'

CARELESS TALK

Performed by Stanley Holloway and Leslie Henson
in 'Up and Doing' (1940)
by Stanley Holloway and Graham John

S.H.   The other day when you and I were lowering a Bass,
           We looked upon a poster from a drawing by Fougasse,
L.H.   And someone whispered, 'I know where they've sent
           the Fusiliers,'
           And I said, 'Shut your trap, you fool, remember walls
           have ears.'

Unison   Careless talk lets vital secrets out,
S.H.   You never know who's listening to what you talk
           about.
L.H.   If little Mrs So-and-So announces twins at Felixstowe,
           Lord Haw Haw would at once proclaim
           That Winston Churchill is to blame.

Unison   Careless talk
S.H.   May make you have to pay,
L.H.   You never know who's on your side today.
S.H.   These days of changing Europe many false reports
           abound,
           And idle talk and rumours by the score are to be
           found.
           D'you know what Turkey's up to now?
L.H.   Yes, three and four a pound.
Unison   So be very very careful what you say.

           Careless talk lets vital secrets out,
L.H.   As Mr Stanley Holloway will prove beyond a doubt.
S.H.   A soldier stumbled in a train, I said, 'Pick up tha
           musket, Sam,'
           And Berlin ran with joyful sounds, 'Ze British heff
           laid down their arms.'

Unison	Careless talk
L.H.	May mean the deuce to pay,
S.H.	A honeymooning couple went away.
	The train it left from Chester, in the black-out all was still.
	The bride was kissed and whispered, 'You may do your wicked will.'
L.H.	But the guard had put the bridegroom on the local train to Rhyl.
Unison	So be very very careful what you say.

S.H.	The silly ass who burbles in a tram or in a bus,
	Is telling little Goebbels what he wants to know from us.
L.H.	So as the weather's warmer and the wind is in the south,
	Don't button up your overcoat, just button up your mouth.

Unison	Careless talk lets vital secrets out,
L.H.	The late lamented Anne Boleyn was too inclined to spout.
S.H.	She gossip'd in an idle hour – they bunged her in the Bloody Tower,
	And now it's difficult to charm, with 'er 'ead tucked underneath 'er arm.

Unison	Careless talk
L.H.	May make you have to pay,
	There's a little more taxation on the way.
S.H.	With less allowances we cannot fill the empty pot,
	It really leaves us speechless, discontented with our lot.
L.H.	But how can we get speechless, when it's sixteen bob a bot!
Unison	So be very very careful what you say.

	Careless talk lets vital secrets out,
S.H.	The Joneses expect a visit from the stork without a doubt.
	Of course the Joneses are full of joy, they hoped that it would be a boy,

L.H.   And so they wait from day to day to hear the bird is on
                   its way.

Unison   But a careless stork
S.H.   May mean the deuce to pay,
                When another little stranger's on the way.
                The stork is getting modern and doesn't care a damn,
                When he's very very busy and finds he's in a jam,
L.H.   Drops the new recruit by parachute, complete with
                 cot and pram.
Unison   So be very very very very very very very very very
                 very careful what you say.

GET ME TO THE CHURCH ON TIME
Words by Alan Jay Lerner (1956)
Music by Frederick Loewe

I'm getting married in the morning
Ding! dong! the bells are gonna chime,
Pull out the stopper;
Let's have a whopper;
But get me to the church on time.

I gotta be there in the morning
Spruced up and looking in my prime.
Girls, come and kiss me;
Show how you'll miss me;
But get me to the church on time.

If I am dancing,
Roll up the floor!
If I am whistling
Whewt me out the door!
(*Whistle*)

30

For I'm getting married in the morning,
Ding! dong! the bells are gonna chime.
Kick up a rumpus,
But don't lose the compass;
And get me to the church,
Get me to the church,
For Pete's sake
Get me to the church on time!

COMEDY TONIGHT
by Stephen Sondheim (1964)

Something familiar, something peculiar,
Something for ev'ryone, a comedy tonight!
Something appealing, something appalling,
Something for ev'ryone, a comedy tonight!
Nothing with kings, nothing with crowns,
Bring on the lovers, liars and clowns!
Old situations, new complications,
Nothing portentous or polite,
Tragedy tomorrow, comedy tonight!

Something convulsive, something repulsive,
Something for ev'ryone, a comedy tonight!
Something esthetic, something frenetic,
Something for ev'ryone, a comedy tonight!
Nothing of Gods, nothing of Fate,
Weighty affairs will just have to wait.
Nothing that's formal, nothing that's normal,
No recitations to recite!
Open the curtain, comedy tonight!

WIV A LITTLE BIT OF LUCK
Words by Alan Jay Lerner (1956)
Music by Frederick Loewe

The Lord above gave man an arm of iron,
So he could do his job and never shirk.
The Lord above gave man an arm of iron
But wiv a little bit of luck, wiv a little bit of luck,
Someone else'll do the blinkin' work.
Wiv a little bit, wiv a little bit,
Wiv a little bit of luck you'll never work.

The Lord above made man to help his neighbour,
No matter where, on land or sea and foam.
The Lord above made man to help his neighbour
But wiv a little bit of luck, wiv a little bit of luck,
When he comes around you won't be home.
Wiv a little bit, wiv a little bit,
Wiv a little bit of luck you won't be home.

Oh, you can walk the straight and narrow,
But wiv a little bit of luck you'll run amok.

The gentle sex was made for man to marry,
To tend his needs and see his food is cooked.
The gentle sex was made for man to marry
But wiv a little bit of luck, wiv a little bit of luck,
You can have it all and not get hooked.
Wiv a little bit, wiv a little bit,
Wiv a little bit of luck you won't get hooked.
Wiv a little bit, wiv a little bit,
Wiv a little bit of blooming luck.

LONDON PRIDE

Performed by Stanley Holloway at the Phoenix Theatre (1969)
by Noël Coward

London Pride has been handed down to us,
London Pride is a flower that's free,
London Pride means our own dear town to us,
And our pride it forever will be.
Woa Liza see the coster barrows,
Vegetable marrows and the fruit piled high.
Woa Liza little London sparrows,
Covent Garden Market where the costers cry.
Cockney feet mark the beat of history,
Ev'ry street pins a memory down.
Nothing ever can quite replace
The grace of London Town.

Refrain
There's a little city flow'r every spring unfailing,
Growing in the crevices by some London railing.
Tho' it has a Latin name in town and countryside,
We in England call it London Pride.

London Pride has been handed down to us
London Pride is a flower that's free,
London Pride means our own dear town to us,
And our pride it forever will be.
Hey lady when the day is dawning
See the p'liceman yawning on his lonely beat.
Gay lady, Mayfair in the morning
Hear the footsteps echo in the empty street.
Early rain and the pavements glistening
All Park Lane in a shimmering gown.
Nothing ever could break or harm
The charm of London Town.

In our city darkened now street and squares and crescent,
We can feel our living past in our shadowed present.
Ghosts beside our starlit Thames who lived and loved and died,
Keep throughout the ages London Pride.

London Pride has been handed down to us,
London Pride is a flower that's free,
London Pride means our own dear town to us,
And our pride it forever will be.
Grey city stubbornly implanted
Taken so for granted for a thousand years.
Stay city smokily enchanted
Cradle of our memories and hopes and fears.
Ev'ry blitz your resistance toughening
From the Ritz to the Anchor and Crown
Nothing ever could over ride
The pride of London Town.

PART III

Music-Hall Performers

MY LORD TOMNODDY
Various performers (early nineteenth century)

My Lord Tomnoddy got up one day
And his Lordship rang for his cabriolet.
Tiger Tim was clean of limb,
His boots were polished, his jacket was trim,
With a very smart tie, his smart cravat,
And a smart cockade on the top of his hat.
Tallest of boys or shortest of men
He stood in his stockings just four feet ten,
And he asked as he held the door on the swing,
'Pray did your Lordship please to ring?'
'Yes, Tiger Tim. Come, tell me true,
What may a nobleman find to do?'
Tim bit his lip, Tim scratched his head,
Tim let go the handle and thus Tim said,
As the door released behind him banged,
'An't please you, me Lord, there's a man to be hanged.'
My Lord Tomnoddy jumped up at the news
And ran to Sir Carnaby Jenks at the Blues.
Took a squint at his watch. Half past two.
So he ran to MacHughes and Lieutenant Tragoo.
'Rope dancers a score I've seen before,
Madam Sacci and Master Blackmore,

But to see a man swing at the end of a string,
With his neck in a noose, would be quite a new thing.'
My Lord Tomnoddy stepped into his cab,
'Twas dark rifle green with a lining of drab,
Through street and through square his high-trotting mare,
Like one of Ducrow's goes pawing the air,
And down Piccadilly and Waterloo Place
Went the high-trotting mare at the deuce of a pace.
She produced some alarm but she didn't do harm,
Save frightening a nurse with a child on her arm;
Knocking down very much to the sweeper's dismay,
An old woman who wouldn't get out of the way;
Upsetting a stall near Exeter Hall,
Which made all the pious church mission folks squawl.
Now eastward afar through Temple Bar
My Lord Tomnoddy directs his car,
Never heeding their squawls, their calls or their bawls,
And merely just catching a glimpse of St Paul's,
Turns down the Old Bailey in front of the jail, he
Pulls up to the door of a gin shop and gaily
Cries: 'What must I fork out tonight, my trump,
For the whole first floor of the "Magpie and Stump"?'
The clock struck twelve, 'tis dark midnight,
But the 'Magpie and Stumps' one blaze of light.
The parties are met, the tables are set,
There's punch, cold without, hot within, heavy wet,
Ale glasses and jugs and rummers and mugs,
And sand on the floor without carpet or rugs,
Cold fowl and cigars, pickled onions in jars,
Welsh rarebits and kidneys, rare work for the jaws.
The clock struck one, supper is done,
Sir Carnaby Jenks is full of his fun.
My Lord Tomnoddy is drinking gin toddy,
And laughing and joking at everybody.
All singing and drinking save Captain MacHughes,
Who's dropping his head and taking a snooze.
While Sir Carnaby Jenks is busy at work
Blacking his nose with a piece of burnt cork.
The clock struck two, the clock struck three,
Who's so merry, so merry as we?
The clock struck four, round the debtor's door
Are gathered a couple of thousand or more.

The clock struck five, the sheriffs arrive,
And the crowd is so great the street seems alive.
Sir Carnaby Jenks blinks and winks,
A candle burns down in the socket and stinks.
While Lieutenant Tragoo and my Lord Tomnoddy
Are nodding their heads through drinking their toddy.
And just as the dawn is beginning to peep
The whole of the party are fast asleep.
The clock struck nine, the finishing stroke
Then my Lord Tomnoddy awoke,
And Tragoo and Sir Carnaby Jenks arose
And Captain MacHughes and the black on his nose.
'Hello, hello, here's the Devil to pay,
Fellow's been cut down and taken away.
They'll laugh at us and quiz us all over the town,
We're all of us done so uncommonly brown.'
What was to be done? It was perfectly plain,
They couldn't well hang the man over again.
What was to be done? The man was dead.
So my Lord Tomnoddy went home to bed.

GOIN' TO THE DERBY
As performed by J. W. Rowley (1850)

I'm Billy Bell,
A costermonger as you sees,
A-dealin' in carrots, turnips, leeks and cabbages,
Cauliflower and broccoli,
Really I may say.
I deals in heverything wot's in the vegetable way.
And tho' I work so 'ard I likes me pleasure too
And once a year like other folks the nobby thing can do.
For every Derby day
I dresses up so smart

And drives meself to Hepsom in me little donkey cart.
Yus, I'm up wiv th' lark that mornin'
And up to all sorts of larks all day.
It aint no 'ardship for me t' get up early
I'm as wide awake then as at any other time.
With the first of the vehicles you'll see me on the road.

Chorus
Goin' to the Derby,
Lookin' very smart,
Doin' all the journey in me donkey cart.
Passin' all the vehicles
Like a bloomin' dart,
Goin' to the Derby in me little donkey cart.

And when I gets to Hepsom
Amongst the bustle there,
I puts away me donkey
What 'asn't turned a hair.
Then I gets me luncheon,
A chunk of bread and cheese
With a gallon jar of fourpenny, oh! at which you wouldn't sneeze.
And while I sits enjoyin'
Me very 'umble fare,
I sees the swells their shammy and their nobby things prepare.
But they doesn't eat an' drink with a better 'eart
Then me wot goes to Hepsom in me little donkey cart.
Ah then when I gets 'ome
I give Billy 'is supper (that's me)
And Tommy a rub dahn (that's me donkey)
Tumbles into me virtuous couch.
Up in the mornin' to work a-sellin' me vegetables
And go there like a good 'un till the time comes round again.
And every year if you look out for me you'll see me –

Chorus
Goin' to the Derby,
Lookin' very smart,
Doin' all the journey in me donkey cart.
Passin' all the vehicles
Like a bloomin' dart,
Goin' to the Derby in me little donkey cart.

40

THE DARK GIRL DRESS'D IN BLUE
Written and performed by Harry Clifton (1862)

From a village away in Leicestershire,
To London here I came,
To see the Exhibition and
All places of great fame.
But what I suffer'd since I came,
I now will tell to you.
How I lost my heart and senses too,
Thro' a dark girl dress'd in blue.

Chorus
She was a fine girl, fol de riddle I do
A charmer, fol de riddle eh.

'Twas on a Friday morning
The first day of August,
When of that day I ever think
My heart feels ready to bust.
I went in a sixpenny omnibus,
To the Exhibition of Sixty-two,
On a seat by the right hand side of the door
Sat a dark girl dress'd in blue.

Chorus

When we arriv'd in the Brompton Road,
The Lady look'd so strange,
The conductor he said, 'Sixpence, Ma'am,'
Said she, 'I have no change.
I've nothing less than a five pound note,
Whatever shall I do?'
Said I, 'Allow me to pay.' 'Oh thank you, sir!'
Said the dark girl dress'd in blue.

Chorus

41

We chatted and talk'd as we onward walk'd
About one thing or the other,
She ask'd me too, oh wasn't it kind?
If I had a father or mother.
Oh yes, says I, and a grandmother too;
But pray, miss, what are you?
'Oh I'm chief engineer in a Milliner's Shop,'
Says the dark girl dress'd in blue.

Chorus

We walk'd about for an hour or two,
Thro' building near and far,
Till we came to the grand refreshment room,
I went straight up to the bar.
She slipp'd in my hand a five pound note.
I said, 'What are you going to do?'
'Oh don't think it strange I must have change,'
Said the dark girl dress'd in blue.

Chorus

I call'd a waiter and handed him the note
And said, 'Please change me that.'
The waiter bow'd and touch'd his hair
For this waiter wore no hat.
In silver and gold five pounds he brought
I gave him coppers a few,
And the change of the note I then did hand
To the dark girl dress'd in blue.

Chorus

She thank'd me and said, 'I must away,
Farewell till we meet again,
For I've got to go to Pimlico
To catch the Brighton train.'
She quickly glided from my sight
And soon was lost to view.
I turn'd to leave when by my side
Stood a tall man dress'd in blue.

Chorus

This tall man said, 'Excuse me, sir,
I'm one of the X division,
That note was bad, my duty is
To take you on suspicion.'
Said I, 'For a Lady I obtain'd the change.'
He said, 'Are you telling me true?
Where's she live? What's her name?' Says I, 'I don't know,
She was a dark girl dress'd in blue.'

Chorus

My story they believ'd, they thought I'd been deceiv'd,
But they said I must hand back the cash.
I thought 'twas a sin as I gave them the tin
And away went five pounds smash.
So all young men take my advice
Be careful what you do
When you make the acquaintance of ladies strange,
Especially a 'dark girl dress'd in blue'.

Chorus
She was a fine girl, fol de riddle I do
A charmer, fol de riddle eh.

ACT ON THE SQUARE BOYS
As performed by The Great Vance (Alfred Peck Stevens), 1866

Thro' being fond of acting right,
Straightforward, just and fair,
I try to make my troubles light,
And little do I care.
As happy as a king I live,
On just what I can spare,

And from experience I give
This hint, act on the square.

Refrain
Act on the square, boys,
Act on the square,
Upright and fair, boys,
Act on the square . . .
Act on the square, boys,
Act on the square,
Upright and fair, boys,
Act on the square.

Now in the street, a thing so bad,
Which often is the case,
A swellish, foolish-looking lad,
Some modest girl will chase.
Then square you round and let him see
If he annoyance dare,
You'll give him striking proof to shew,
How to act on the square.

Refrain

When out one night with noisy swells,
Th' Haymarket kept alive,
One Serjeant X with oyster shells,
To pelt they did contrive.
They nearly got into disgrace,
But squaring served them there,
And brightly shone the Bobby's face,
Who liked to see things square.

Refrain

I never liked a round game, nay,
Round tables can't abear,
And in a circus I can't stay,
So I live in a Square.
Now Brothers all and Masons too,
Of good let's do our share,

And when a chance presents itself,
We must act on the square.

Refrain
Act on the square, boys,
Act on the square,
Upright and fair, boys,
Act on the square . . .
Act on the square, boys,
Act on the square,
Upright and fair, boys,
Act on the square.

A MOTTO FOR EVERY MAN

As performed by Arthur Lloyd (late nineteenth century)

Some people you've met in your time no doubt
Who've never looked happy or gay,
I'll tell you the way to get jolly and stout
If you'll listen a while to my lay.
I've come here to tell you a bit of my mind,
And please with the same if I can.
Advice in my song you will certainly find
And a motto for every man.

So we will sing
And banish melancholy.
Trouble may come,
We'll do the best we can
To drive care away
For grieving is a folly.
Put your shoulder to the wheel
Is a motto for every man.

We cannot all fight in this battle of life
The weak must go to the wall.
So do to each other the thing that is right
For there's room in this world for us all.
Credit refuse if you've money to pay
You'll find it the wiser plan,
And a penny laid by for a rainy day
Is a motto for every man.

Drive care away
For grieving is a folly,
Put your shoulder to the wheel
Is a motto for every man.
Economy study but don't be mean
A penny may lose a pound,
Through this world a conscience clean
Will carry you safe and sound.

It's all very well to be free, I own,
To do a good turn when you can.
But charity always commences at home,
There's a motto for every man.

So we will sing
And banish melancholy;
Trouble may come,
We'll do the best we can
To drive care away
For grieving is a folly.
Put your shoulder to the wheel
Is a motto for every man.

I LIVE IN TRAFALGAR SQUARE
(The Optimistic Outcast)

As performed by Morney Cash (1902)
by C. W. Murphy

Today I've been busy removing,
And I'm all of a 'fidgety-fidge',
My last 'digs' were on the Embankment,
The third seat from Waterloo Bridge!
But the cooking and, oh! the attendance,
Didn't happen to suit me so well,
So I ordered my man to pack up, and
Look out for another hotel.
He did, and the new place is 'extra' I vow!
Just wait till I tell you where I'm staying now:

Chorus
I live in Trafalgar Square,
With four lions to guard me.
Fountains and statues all over the place,
And the 'Metropole' staring me right in the face!
I'll own it's a trifle draughty,
But I look at it this way, you see,
If it's good enough for Nelson,
It's quite good enough for me!

The beds ain't as soft as they might be,
Still the temp'rature's never too high!
And it's nice to see swells who are passing
Look on you with envious eye.
And then when you wake in the morning
Just fancy how nice it must be,
To have a good walk for your breakfast,
And the same for your dinner and tea!
There's many a swell up in Park Lane tonight,
Who'd be glad if he only had my appetite.

Chorus

49

When I think of those unlucky bounders,
The Morgans and Clarence de Clares,
Who are forced to put up at the 'Cecil',
My tenderest sympathy's theirs!
And to show I'm not selfish or greedy,
I just tell each aristocrat,
That I don't mind exchanging apartments,
Now, I can't say fairer than that!
But the soft-headed sillies won't hear what I say,
They still go on suff'ring while I'm all OK!

Chorus
I live in Trafalgar Square,
With four lions to guard me.
Fountains and statues all over the place,
And the 'Metropole' staring me right in the face!
I'll own it's a trifle draughty,
But I look at it this way, you see,
If it's good enough for Nelson,
It's quite good enough for me!

BURLINGTON BERTIE FROM BOW

As performed by Ella Shields (1914)
by William Hargreaves

I'm Bert, p'raps you've heard of me,
Bert, you've had word of me,
Jogging along, hearty and strong,
Living on plates of fresh air.
I dress up in fashion, and
When I am feeling depress'd,
I shave from my cuff, all the whiskers and fluff,
Stick my hat on and toddle up West.

Chorus

I'm Burlington Bertie, I rise at ten-thirty,
And saunter along like a toff.
I walk down the Strand with my gloves on my hand,
Then I walk down again with them off.
I'm all airs and graces, correct easy paces,
Without food so long, I've forgot where my face is,
I'm Bert, Bert, I haven't a shirt,
But my people are well off, you know.
Nearly ev'ryone knows me, from Smith to Lord Roseb'ry,
I'm Burlington Bertie from Bow!

I stroll with Lord Hurlington,
Roll, in the Burlington,
Call for Champagne, walk out again,
Come back and borrow the ink.
I live most expensive,
Like Tom Lipton I'm in the swim.
He's got so much 'oof', that he sleeps on the roof,
And I live in the room over him.

Chorus

I'm Burlington Bertie, I rise at ten-thirty,
Then saunter along Temple Bar.
As round there I skip, I keep shouting 'Pip, Pip!'
And the darn'd fools think I'm in my car.
At Rothschild's I swank it, my body I plank it,
On his front doorstep with the *Mail* for a blanket.
I'm Bert, Bert, and Rothschild was hurt,
He said 'You can't sleep there.' I said, 'Oh!'
He said, 'I'm Rothschild, sonny!' I said, 'That's damn'd funny,
I'm Burlington Bertie from Bow!'

I smile condescendingly,
While they're extending me.
Cheer upon cheer, when I appear,
Captain with my Polo team.
So strict are my people,
They're William the Conqueror's strain,
If they ever knew, I'd been talking to you,
Why, they'd never look at me again.

51

Chorus

I'm Burlington Bertie, I rise at ten-thirty,
And reach Kempton Park about three.
I stand by the rail, when a horse is for sale,
And you ought to see Wooton watch me.
I lean on some awning, while Lord Derby's yawning,
Then he bids 'Two Thousand' and I bid 'Good morning'.
I'm Bert, Bert, I'd buy one, a cert,
But where could I keep it you know!
I can't let my man see me in bed with a gee-gee,
I'm Burlington Bertie from Bow!

My pose, tho' ironical
Shows that my monocle
Holds up my face, keeps it in place,
Stops it from slipping away.
Cigars, I smoke thousands,
I usually deal in the Strand,
But you've got to take care, when you're getting them there,
Or some idiot might stand on your hand.

Chorus

I'm Burlington Bertie, I rise at ten-thirty,
Then Buckingham Palace I view.
I stand in the yard, while they're changing the guard,
And the King shouts across, 'Toodle-oo'.
The Prince of Wales' brother, along with some other,
Slaps me on the back and says, 'Come and see mother.'
I'm Bert, Bert, and Royalty's hurt,
When they ask me to dine, I say, 'No! I've just had a Banana with
    Lady Diana,
I'm Burlington Bertie from Bow!'

OH, I MUST GO HOME TONIGHT!
As performed by Billy Williams (1908)
by William Hargreaves

Jones was a fellow who went the pace with all his youthful might,
    And took a great delight in staying out all night.
When people were thinking of going to bed, around the West he'd
    roam,
He'd go to Clubs or go to Pubs, but never would go home.
But one night inside the club he gave his pals a fright,
When he said, 'I'm going home,' and wished them all Goodnight.
They thought that he was joking and they all laughed out aloud,
But Jones looked very serious as he shouted to the crowd.

Chorus
'Oh I must go home tonight, I must go home tonight,
I don't care if it's snowing, blowing, I'm going,
I only got married this morning and it fills me with delight.
I'll stay out as long as you like next week,
But I must go home tonight!'

Off to the station he made a dash, to ask about his train,
To take him home again – but he asked all in vain.
They said there's none running at all tonight to where you want
    to go,
All traffic is suspended for the line's blocked up with snow.
He walked up and down the platform anything but gay,
Said he, 'I would tramp home if I only knew the way.'
A porter said, 'You'll have to wait till morning, I'm afraid.'
But Jones said, 'That's impossible I cannot be delayed.'

Chorus

Out of the station he made a dive, and in the street did land,
He yelled and waved his hand, for a taxi off the stand.
He gave his address to the driver, and in confidence agreed
To give him half a sov'reign if he put on extra speed.

But smash went the taxi, for the speed was far too high,
Said Jones, 'I don't live up here,' as he shot in the sky.
He fell down on the pavement, and a P'liceman said below,
'We'll take you to the hospital,' but Jonesy whispered, 'No.'

Chorus
'Oh I must go home tonight, I must go home tonight,
I don't care if it's snowing, blowing, I'm going,
I only got married this morning and it fills me with delight.
I'll stay out as long as you like next week,
But I must go home tonight!'

I THOWT MEBBE I WOULD – AN' I DID

As performed by Jack Pleasants (1912)
by Ernest Melvin

I'll never forget
The first time I met
Wi' sweet Annie Stump;
Ba gum! she wor plump!
She come up to me,
'Hey, Willyum,' says she,
'Be's't lookin' for owt?'
Then gave me a clout.
She had such a takin' way,
She took me a walk that day;
An' when wi' that wench
I sat on a bench,
She gave me a squeeze,
An' says, 'Kiss me please!'

Well I looks at 'er,
An' I thinks, 'She's a likely young lass!'
An' I gowps at 'er,

She wor lush as a meadow o' grass.
An' I winks at 'er,
When she says, 'Wil'ta cuddle me, kid?'
An' I thowt – mebbe I would, An' I – well – I did!

It 'appened one night
I got an invite
To Farmer Brown's Ball,
Wi Annie an' all!
She looked a real treat,
As red as a beet,
An' bloomin' like some Ger-a-ni-i-um.
It fair made me swell wi' pride
To 'ave that lass by my side.
We danced yan, an' then
I blushed at 'er when
She said with a pout,
'Let's sit next yan out!'

Well I looks at 'er
An' I thinks, 'She's a likely young lass!'
An' I gowps at 'er,
As we waited for dancers to pass.
An' I winks at 'er,
When she says, 'Let's sit where we'll be hid!'
An' I thowt mebbe I would,
An' I – well – I did!

She 'olded my 'and,
And said, 'Ain't it grand
To sit like this 'ere.'
Ba gum! I felt queer.
An' then she says, 'Will
You marry me, Bill?'
I 'ardly could speak!
She 'ad got a cheek.
An' soon to the church I was led,
Where Parson stood waitin' to wed.
An' next thing I knew,
He ask'd me, 'Will you
Take 'er for your wife?
Your trouble an' strife?'

Well I looks at 'er,
An' I thinks, 'She's a likely young lass!'
An' I gowps at 'er,
For I'd 'eard she'd got plenty o' brass.
An' I winks at 'er,
When to put on the ring I was bid,
An' I thowt mebbe I would,
An' I – well, – I did!

I WENT DOWN TO BRIGHT

by Phil Ray (1912)

I was not feelin' right!
So I went down to Bright . . .
To spend a few mins by the sea.
On Victoria plat . . .
I patiently sat
With my little port-mant on me knee.
We reached Clapham Junc
At three thirty punc . . .
As the train shunted into the Stash . . .
Said the Guard 'Make a start
Room for one, this compart' . . .
I said, 'Thanks for your kind informash' . . .
I had just settled down
When in dashed Aggie Brown –
Aggie Brown in the sere and the yell
Her age is uncert . . .
She's at least eight and thirt . . .
And she's broad round the Marie Corell
I felt a bit nerve . . .
As she started to swerve . . .
She said: 'Men, must I stand here alone?'

Then she glared round at me
And sat flop on me knee
Right on the spur of the mom . . .
So I adjourned . . . to Ostend
Met a congene lady friend
And we posed as wart nymphs on the rocks.
She'd a rather swag rig
And a very fine fig . . .
And her hair was no strange to perox . . .
As we strolled in the brine
I said, 'What's the time?'
Her behaviour was somewhat unuse . . .
She looked rather askance
At me fairly short pants
So I bobbed down to hide my confuse . . .

CHAMPAGNE CHARLIE

Original lyrics by George Leybourne (1866)
Revised lyrics by Ernest Irving and Frank Eyton (1944)

Some people go for funny drinks and down 'em by the pail,
Like coffee, cocoa, tea and milk and even Adam's ale;
For my part they can keep the lot I never would complain,
I wouldn't touch the bloomin' stuff, I only drink champagne.
For . . .

Chorus
Champagne Charlie is my name,
Champagne drinking is my game,
There's no drink as good as fizz! fizz! fizz!
I'll drink ev'ry drop there is! is! is!
All round town it is the same,
By Pop! Pop! Pop! I rose to fame.

I'm the idol of the barmaids,
And Champagne Charlie is my name.

I earned my famous title thro' a hobby which I've got,
Of never letting others pay however long the shot;
Whoever drinks at my expense has no need to complain,
For ev'ryone I treat alike I make them drink champagne.
For . . .

Chorus

Perhaps you think what I say now is just a bit of chaff,
And only put into this song to raise a little laugh;
To prove that I'm not jesting and the sort of man I am,
I'm goin' to stand champagne all round and stand it like a lamb.
For . . .

Chorus
Champagne Charlie is my name,
Champagne drinking is my game,
There's no drink as good as fizz! fizz! fizz!
I'll drink ev'ry drop there is! is! is!
All round town it is the same,
By Pop! Pop! Pop! I rose to fame.
I'm the idol of the barmaids,
And Champagne Charlie is my name.

PART IV

Humorous Poetry

(Recorded in 1960)

HOW PLEASANT TO KNOW MR LEAR
by Edward Lear

How pleasant to know Mr Lear!
   Who has written such volumes of stuff!
Some think him ill-tempered and queer,
   But a few think him pleasant enough.

His mind is concrete and fastidious,
   His nose is remarkably big;
His visage is more or less hideous,
   His beard it resembles a wig.

He has ears, and two eyes, and ten fingers,
   Leastways if you reckon two thumbs;
Long ago he was one of the singers,
   But now he is one of the dumbs.

He sits in a beautiful parlour,
   With hundreds of books on the wall;
He drinks a great deal of Marsala,
   But never gets tipsy at all.

He has many friends, laymen and clerical;
   Old Foss is the name of his cat;

His body is perfectly spherical,
   He weareth a runcible hat.

When he walks in a waterproof white,
   The children run after him so!
Calling out, 'He's come out in his night-
   Gown, that crazy old Englishman, oh!'

He weeps by the side of the ocean,
   He weeps on the top of the hill;
He purchases pancakes and lotion,
   And chocolate shrimps from the mill.

He reads but he cannot speak Spanish,
   He cannot abide ginger-beer:
Ere the days of his pilgrimage vanish,
   How pleasant to know Mr Lear!

THE APE AND THE LADY
by W. S. Gilbert

A Lady fair, of lineage high,
Was loved by an Ape, in the days gone by –
The Maid was radiant as the sun,
The Ape was a most unsightly one –
   So it would not do –
   His scheme fell through;
For the Maid, when his love took formal shape,
   Expressed such terror
   At his monstrous error,
That he stammered an apology and made his 'scape,
The picture of a disconcerted Ape.

With a view to rise in the social scale,
He shaved his bristles, and he docked his tail,
He grew moustachios, and he took his tub,
   And he paid a guinea to a toilet club.
   But it would not do,
   The scheme fell through –
For the Maid was Beauty's fairest Queen,
   With golden tresses,
   Like a real princess's,
While the Ape, despite his razor keen,
Was the apiest Ape that ever was seen!

He bought white ties, and he bought dress suits,
He crammed his feet into bright tight boots,
And to start his life on a brand-new plan,
He christened himself Darwinian Man!
   But it would not do,
   The scheme fell through –
For the Maiden fair, whom the monkey craved,
   Was a radiant Being,
   With a brain far-seeing –
While a Man, however well-behaved,
At best is only a monkey-shaved!

THE YARN OF THE 'NANCY BELL'

by W. S. Gilbert

'Twas on the shores that round our coast
   From Deal to Ramsgate span,
That I found alone on a piece of stone
   An elderly naval man.

His hair was weedy, his beard was long,
  And weedy and long was he,
And I heard this wight on the shore recite,
  In a singular minor key:

'Oh, I am a cook and a captain bold,
  And the mate of the *Nancy* brig,
And a bo'sun tight, and a midshipmite,
  And the crew of the captain's gig.'

And he shook his fists and he tore his hair,
  Till I really felt afraid,
For I couldn't help thinking the man had been drinking,
  And so I simply said:

'Oh, elderly man, it's little I know
  Of the duties of men of the sea,
But I'll eat my hand if I understand
  How you can possibly be.

'At once a cook, and a captain bold,
  And the mate of the *Nancy* brig,
And a bo'sun tight, and a midshipmite,
  And the crew of the captain's gig.'

Then he gave a hitch to his trousers, which
  Is a trick all seamen larn,
And having got rid of a thumping quid,
  He spun this painful yarn:

''Twas in the good ship *Nancy Bell*
  That we sailed to the Indian sea,
And there on a reef we come to grief,
  Which has often occurred to me.

'And pretty nigh all o' the crew was drowned
  (There was seventy-seven o' soul),
And only ten of the *Nancy*'s men
  Said 'Here!' to the muster-roll.

'There was me and the cook and the captain bold.
  And the mate of the *Nancy* brig,

And the bo'sun tight, and a midshipmite,
    And the crew of the captain's gig.

'For a month we'd neither wittles nor drink,
    Till a-hungry we did feel,
So we drawed a lot, and accordin' shot
    The captain for our meal.

'The next lot fell to the *Nancy*'s mate,
    And a delicate dish he made;
Then our appetite with the midshipmite
    We seven survivors stayed.

'And then we murdered the bo'sun tight,
    And he much resembled pig;
Then we wittled free, did the cook and me,
    On the crew of the captain's gig.

'Then only the cook and me was left,
    And the delicate question, "Which
Of us two goes to the kettle?" arose
    And we argued it out as sich.

'For I loved that cook as a brother, I did,
    And the cook he worshipped me;
But we'd both be blowed if we'd either be stowed
    In the other chap's hold, you see.

'"I'll be eat if you dines off me," says Tom,
    "Yes, that," says I, "you'll be," –
"I'm boiled if I die, my friend," quoth I,
    And "Exactly so," quoth he.

'Says he, "Dear James, to murder me
    Were a foolish thing to do,
For don't you see that you can't cook *me*,
    While I can – and will – cook *you*!"

'So he boils the water, and takes the salt
    And the pepper in proportions true
(Which he never forgot), and some chopped shalot,
    And some sage and parsley too.

' "Come here," says he, with a proper pride,
    Which his smiling features tell,
" 'Twill soothing be if I let you see,
    How extremely nice you'll smell."

'And he stirred it round and round and round,
    And he sniffed at the foaming broth;
When I ups with his heels, and smothers his squeals
    In the scum of the boiling broth.

'And I eat that cook in a week or less,
    And – as I eating be
The last of his chops, why, I almost drops,
    For a wessel in sight I see!

'And I never grieve, and I never smile,
    And I never larf nor play,
But I sit and croak, and a single joke
    I have – which is to say:

'Oh, I am a cook and a captain bold,
    And the mate of the *Nancy* brig,
And a bo'sun tight, and a midshipmite,
    And the crew of the captain's gig!'

PETER THE WAG

by W. S. Gilbert

Policeman Peter Forth I drag
    From his obscure retreat:
He was a merry, genial wag,
    Who loved a mad conceit.

If he were asked the time of day
    By country bumpkins green,
He not unfrequently would say,
    'A quarter past thirteen.'

If ever you by word of mouth
    Enquired of Mister Forth
The way to somewhere in the South,
He always sent you North.
With little boys his beat along
    He loved to stop and play;
He loved to send old ladies wrong,
    And teach their feet to stray.

He would in frolic moments, when
    Such mischief bent upon,
Take Bishops up as betting men –
    Bid Ministers move on.
Then all the worthy boys he knew
    He regularly licked,
And always collared people who
    Had had their pockets picked.

He was not naturally bad,
    Or viciously inclined,
But from his early youth he had
    A waggish turn of mind.
The Men of London grimly scowled
    With indignation wild;
The Men of London gruffly growled,
    But Peter calmly smiled.

Against this minion of the Crown
    The swelling murmurs grew –
From Camberwell to Kentish Town –
    From Rotherhithe to Kew.
Still humoured he his wagsome turn,
    And fed in various ways
The coward rage that dared to burn
    But did not dare to blaze.

Still, Retribution has her day
    Although her flight is slow,
One day that Crusher lost his way
    Near Poland Street, Soho.
The haughty youth, too proud to ask,
    To find his way resolved,
And in the tangle of his task
    Got more and more involved.

The Men of London, overjoyed,
    Came there to jeer their foe –
And flocking crowds completely cloyed
    The mazes of Soho.
The news, on telegraphic wires,
    Sped swiftly o'er the lea –
Excursion trains from distant shires
    Brought myriads to see.

For weeks he trod his self-made beats
    Through Newport, Gerrard, Bear,
Greek, Rupert, Frith, Dean, Poland Streets,
    And into Golden Square:
But all, alas, in vain, for when
    He tried to learn the way
Of little boys or grown-up men
    They none of them would say.

Their eyes would flash – their teeth would grind –
    Their lips would tightly curl –
They'd say, 'Thy way thyself must find,
    Thou misdirecting churl!'
And, similarly, also, when
    He tried a foreign friend;
Italians answered, '*Il balen*' –
    The French, '*No comprehend.*'

The Russ would say with gleaming eye
    '*Sevastopol!*' and groan.
The Greek said, '*Typto, typtomai,*
    Typto, typtein, typton.'
To wander thus for many a year
    That Crusher never ceased –

The Men of London dropped a tear,
    Their anger was appeased.

At length exploring gangs were sent
    To find poor Forth's remains –
A handsome grant by Parliament
    Was voted for their pains.
To seek the poor policeman out
    Bold spirits volunteered,
And when at length they solved the doubt
    The Men of London cheered.

And in a yard, dark, dank, and drear,
    They found him, on the floor –
(It leads from Richmond Buildings – near
    The Royalty stage-door.)
With brandy cold and brandy hot
    They plied him, starved and wet,
And made him sergeant on the spot –
    The Men of London's pet!

OLD BARTY

by Douglas Grant (1919)

If you was to travel for miles around 'ere,
An' ask 'oo you loike o' the folks livin' theere,
If they'd 'eard of Old Barty, age four-score an' ten,
As 'ale an' as 'earty as any two men,
Lor' love 'ee,
They'd know me,
I'm well know'd round 'ere!

It's Barty as does the odd jobs at the 'all,
Who'll sweep up you path – is at anyone's call,
On Sunday, at Church, don't 'ee take round the plate?
Yes, an' stare at you 'ard, if so be as you're late!
Lor' love 'ee,
They know me,
I'm well know'd round 'ere!

They tell me our Church be four 'undred year old,
But there ain't no believin' the lies you be told!
I've lived 'ere the longest – 'twas there afore me,
An if I can't be sartin, then 'ow can they be?
Lor' love 'ee,
They know me,
I'm well know'd round 'ere!

Whenever a lad would a lassie entice,
It's always Old Barty as gives 'im advice:
Says I, 'It's so simple just throw out your chest,
Then look sort o' longin' an' she'll do the rest!'
Lor' love 'ee,
I know 'em,
It's all done so nice!

But now I am old an' my time's gettin' near,
An' life bain't the same now this many a year;
I can 'ear voices callin' most every day,
But I reckon I knows what our Parson will say:
Lord, take 'im,
Yes, take 'im!
'E's well know'd round 'ere!

Discography

(*Note*: Unless otherwise indicated, all records listed are Long Playing Records. Early recordings are denoted by the addition of 78 rpm.)

Part I – MONOLOGUES

And Yet I Don't Know!/'My Word! You Do Look Queer!' New York, 1957. 'Ere's 'Olloway Album. Orchestra conducted by Arthur Lief. Philips BBL 7237 and CBS (Realm) RM 52066
London, 1975. Life in the Old Dog Yet Album. With Alan Cohen and Orchestra and Chris March (piano). ARGO ZDA 170.

Eving's Dorg 'Ospital New York, 1957. 'Ere's 'Olloway Album. Orchestra conducted by Arthur Lief. Philips BBL 7237 and CBS (Realm) RM 52066.

The Street Watchman's Story/On Strike With Concert Party Four (vocal chorus) and Arthur Lief (piano) Riverside RLP 12-824.

Part II – MUSICAL COMEDY PERFORMANCES

It'll Be All the Same New York, 1957. 'Ere's 'Olloway Album. Orchestra conducted by Arthur Lief. Philips BBL 7237 and CBS (Realm) RM 52066.

The King who Wanted Jam for Tea New York, November 1957. With Concert Party Four (vocal chorus) and Arthur Lief (piano). Riverside RLP 12-824.

Sometimes I'm Happy London, 29 November 1927. Duet with Ivy Tresmand. Accompanied by the London Hippodrome Orchestra. Columbia 4651 (78 rpm).
London, 1973. Re-issued by World Record Club (S) H 176 in 'Hit the Deck' Musical Selection and Columbia SX 6551 'Theatreland Show-stoppers'.

Keep Smiling London, 16 April 1934. Accompanied by Drury Lane Theatre Orchestra. Columbia DB 1373 (78 rpm).
London, 1973. Re-issued on World Record Club (S) H 171 – 'Jerome Kern in London'.

My Missus London, 11 March 1940. Columbia FB 2408 (78 rpm).

Careless Talk London, 29 October 1940. Columbia DB 1935 (78 rpm).

Get Me to the Church on Time New York, May 1958. With Broadway Chorus and Orchestra conducted by Fritz Allers. Columbia OL 5090, CBS EPG 68001, BRG 70005, Philips BBE 12252 and RBL 1000 (UK).
London, 1958. With London Cast and Orchestra conducted by Cyril Ornadel. CBS SBRG 70005 and Philips SRBL 1001.
Hollywood, 1964. Film Soundtrack with Chorus and Orchestra conducted by Andre Previn. Columbia 8000 and DBS BRG 72237/BRG 70000.

Wiv a Little Bit of Luck New York, May 1958. With Gordon Dilworth, Rod Maclinnon and Broadway Orchestra conducted by Fritz Allers. Columbia OL 5090, CBS EPG 68001, BRG 70005, Philips BBE 12252 and RBL 1000 (UK).
London, 1958. With Alan Dudley, Bob Chisholm and Drury Lane Orchestra. CBS SBRG 70005 and Philips SRBL 1001.
Hollywood, 1964. Film Soundtrack with Chorus and Orchestra conducted by Andre Previn. Columbia 8000 and CBS BRG 72237/BRG 70000.

Comedy Tonight/London Pride London, July 1964. 'Stanley, I Presume' Album. With the Lisa Grey Singers and Orchestra conducted by Geoff Love. Columbia 33CX 1656, SCXX 3528.

Part III – MUSIC-HALL PERFORMANCES

My Lord Tomnoddy, Goin' to the Derby, Act on the Square Boys, A Motto for Every Man, Champagne Charlie London, 1963. Champagne Charlie Album compiled by Charles Chilton, with Orchestra and Chorus conducted by Alfred Ralston. World Record Club T 325.

The Dark Girl Dress'd in Blue London, April/May 1959. With accompaniment directed by Laurie Johnson. Decca F 11140.

I Live in Trafalgar Square/Oh, I Must Go Home Tonight! New York, 1957. 'Ere's 'Olloway Album. Orchestra conducted by Arthur Lief. Philips BBE 12326/BBL 7256. CBS (Realm) RM 52066.

Burlington Bertie from Bow London, July 1964. 'Stanley, I Presume' Album. With Orchestra conducted by Geoff Love. Columbia 33CX 1656/SCX 3528.

I Thowt Mebbe I Would London, 18 October 1929. Orchestral accompaniment conducted by Philip Lewis. Decca F 1875 (78 rpm). New version with Concert Party Four (Vocal chorus) and Arthur Lief (piano). Riverside RLF 12-824.

Part IV – HUMOROUS POETRY

Edward Lear London, 1960. Caedmon TCE 1049/TC 1078.

The Bab Ballads London, 1960. Caedmon TCE 1104 and TCE 145/146.